CELLO PART | VOL. 8

CELLO SCHOOL

Volume 8
Cello Part
Revised Edition

© 2003, 1991, 1982 Dr. Shinichi Suzuki
Sole publisher for the entire world except Japan:
Summy-Birchard, Inc.
Exclusive print rights administered by
Alfred Publishing Co., Inc.
All rights reserved. Printed in USA.

ISBN-10: 0-7579-2486-7
ISBN-13: 978-0-7579-2486-6

The Suzuki name, logo and wheel device
are trademarks of Dr. Shinichi Suzuki
used under exclusive license by Summy-Bichard, Inc.

Any duplication, adaptation or arrangement of the compositions
contained in this collection requires the written consent of the Publisher.
No part of this book may be photocopied or reproduced in any way without permission.
Unauthorized uses are an infringement of the U.S. Copyright Act and are punishable by law.

INTRODUCTION

FOR THE STUDENT: This material is part of the worldwide Suzuki Method® of teaching. The companion recording should be used along with this publication. A piano accompaniment book is also available for this material.

FOR THE TEACHER: In order to be an effective Suzuki teacher, ongoing education is encouraged. Each regional Suzuki association provides teacher development for its membership via conferences, institutes, short-term and long-term programs. In order to remain current, you are encouraged to become a member of your regional Suzuki association, and, if not already included, the International Suzuki Association.

FOR THE PARENT: Credentials are essential for any Suzuki teacher you choose. We recommend you ask your teacher for his or her credentials, especially those related to training in the Suzuki Method®. The Suzuki Method® experience should foster a positive relationship among the teacher, parent and child. Choosing the right teacher is of utmost importance.

To obtain more information about the Suzuki Association in your region, please contact:

International Suzuki Association
www.internationalsuzuki.org

Under the guidance of Dr. Suzuki since 1978, the editing of the Suzuki Cello School is a continuing cooperative effort of the Cello Committees from Talent Education Japan, the European Suzuki Association, and the Suzuki Association of the Americas.

CONTENTS

Sonata in G Major, *Giovanni Battista Sammartini* 4
    Allegro..4
    Grave..7
    Vivace...8

Allegro Appassionato, Op. 43, *Camille Saint-Saëns* 11

Élégie Op. 24, *Gabriel Fauré* 14

Scherzo Op. 12, *Daniel van Goens* 16

NOTE: The ISA Cello Committee recommends that the entire Suite No. 1 in G Major by J. S. Bach be taught before the student completes Book 8.
Editing is at the discretion of the teacher.

Sonata in G major

Giovanni Battista Sammartini
(1698-1775)

Allegro Appassionato
Op. 43

Camille Saint-Saëns
(1835-1921)

*Alternate bowing

Élégie
Op. 24

Gabriel Fauré
(1845-1924)

Molto Adagio

Scherzo
Op. 12

Daniel van Goens
(1904-1930)

Vivace molto e con spirito

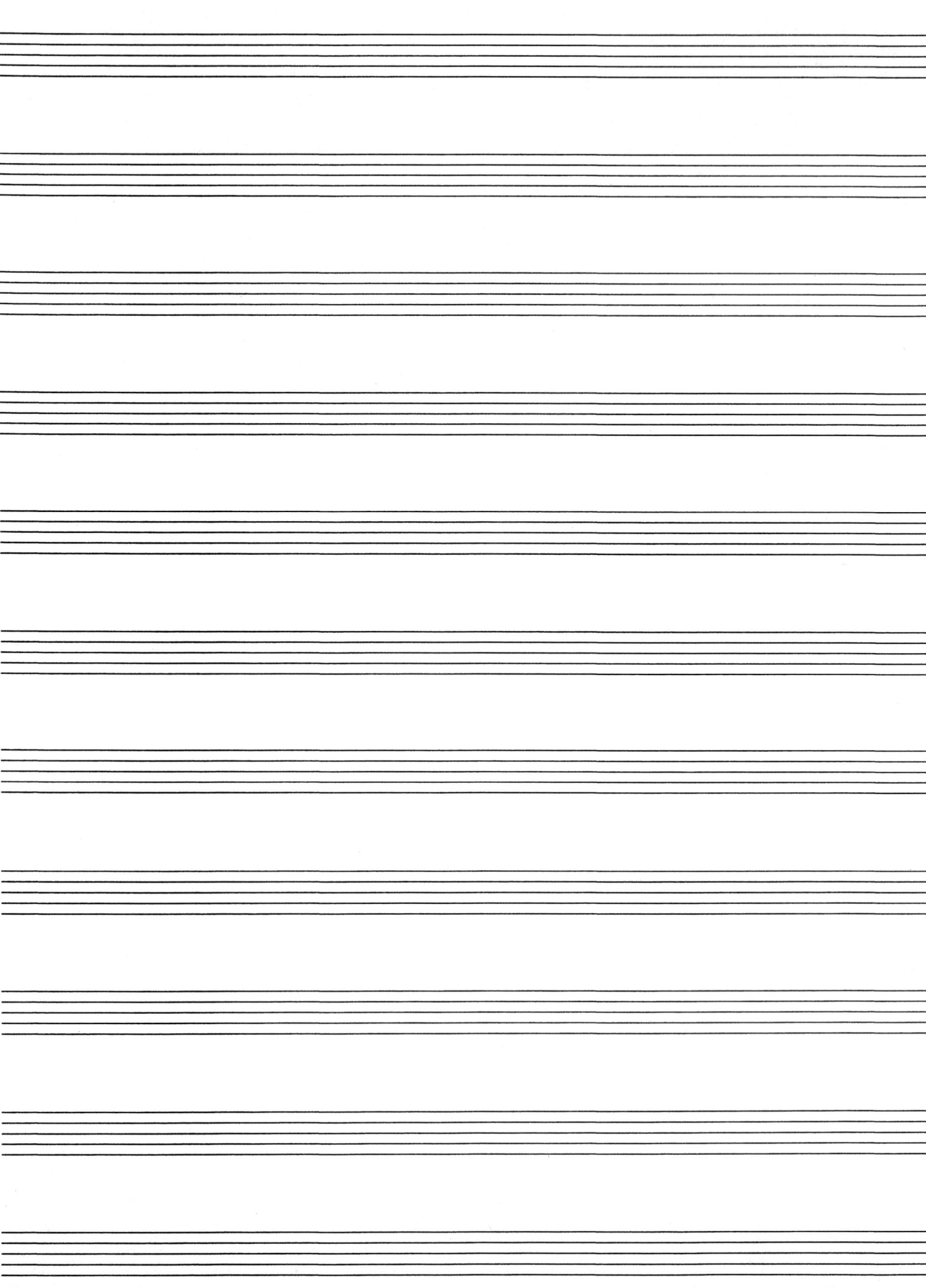